WORDS OF LIFE, LIGHT, AND LOVE

BETTY RAE NICK

EnerPower Press
www.enerpowerpress.com

2011

Copyright © 2011, Betty Rae Nick

Scriptures in italics are from the King James Version.
Scriptures in a regular font are taken from the World English Bible (ebible.org/web).

Unless otherwise credited, pictures are by Iris Lloyd (LPexecutiveservices.com)
The pictures on pages 3, 16, 18, 19, 20, 21, 26, 27 are by Henry Neufeld.
The picture on page 22 is by Gail Olson.

Cover Design: Jason Neufeld (jasonneufelddesign.com)
Cover Photo: Copyright © Mayermiki | Dreamstime.com

ISBN10: 1-893729-98-2
ISBN13: 978-1-893729-98-8

EnerPower Press, an imprint of
Energion Publications
P. O. Box 841
Gonzalez, FL 32560

850-525-3916
www.energionpubs.com

TABLE OF CONTENTS

Preface	iv
God's Unspeakable Gift	1
Christ's Sacrifice	2
God is Seeking for Us	3
The Power of His Love	4
The Only Way	5
Gifts of Enmity Against Sin and Desire for Goodness	6
The Creative Word	7
The New Birth	8
A New Creature	10
Self on the Cross	11
A New Life	13
Heavenly Treasure	15
The Sustaining Word	17
The Mysteries	19
Life Eternal	21
The Rest	22
The Light of Life	23
Our Advocate	24
The Refreshing	25
Victory	26
The Final Victory	27
Dear Reader	28

Preface

This little book has been prepared according to the instruction given in Isaiah 28:10, 12:
   "For precept must be upon precept,
      precept upon precept;
      line upon line, line upon line;
      here a little and there a little:
   "This is the rest wherewith ye shall cause
   the weary to rest; and this is the refreshing."

It is the prayer of the compiler that all who read this little book may be refreshed.

— Betty (Neufeld) Nick

For a double portion, search in the Scriptures, with the use of a concordance, the topics introduced in this book.

Each scripture is printed twice, once in the King James Version (KJV) and then in the World English Bible (WEB), an update of the American Standard Version. The KJV references are in italics, while the WEB references are in regular font. Quotations from Ellen White are in the **Verdana font**. For more information on Ellen White, see page 32.

Some texts are quoted partially. When there is an omission in a text it is marked with an ellipsis (. . .) unless the omission is at the beginning or end. All texts begin with a capital letter and end with a period regardless of original punctuation.

God's Unspeakable Gift

For God so loved the world, that he gave his only begotten Son, that whosoever believeth in him, should not perish but have everlasting life.
— John 3:16

For God so loved the world, that he gave his one and only Son, that whoever believes in him should not perish, but have eternal life. — John 3:16

God was in Christ, reconciling the world unto himself.
— 2 Corinthians 5:19
God was in Christ reconciling the world to himself.
— 2 Corinthians 5:19

> God suffered with His son. In the agony of Gethsemane, the death of Calvary, the heart of infinite Love paid the price of our redemption.
> — SC 13*

No man can come to me, except the Father which hath sent me draw him: and I will raise him up at the last day. — John 6:44
No one can come to me unless the Father who sent me draws him, and I will raise him up in the last day. — John 6:44

---

* See "Dear Reader" on page 28.

Christ's Sacrifice

Let this mind be in you, which was also in Christ Jesus: Who, being in the form of God, thought it not robbery to be equal with God: But made himself of no reputation, and took upon him the form of a servant, and was made in the likeness of men: And being found in fashion as a man, he humbled himself, and became obedient unto death, even the death of the cross. — Philippians 2:5-8

Have this in your mind, which was also in Christ Jesus, who, existing in the form of God, didn't consider equality with God a thing to be grasped, but emptied himself, taking the form of a servant, being made in the likeness of men. And being found in human form, he humbled himself, becoming obedient to death, yes, the death of the cross. — Philippians 2:5-8

Looking unto Jesus the author and finisher of our faith; who for the joy that was set before him endured the cross, . . . lest ye be wearied and faint in your minds. Ye have not yet resisted unto blood, striving against sin. — Hebrews 12:2-4

Looking to Jesus, the author and perfecter of faith, who for the joy that was set before him endured the cross, . . . that you don't grow weary, fainting in your souls. You have not yet resisted to blood, striving against sin. — Hebrews 12:2-4

God is Seeking for Us

Canst thou by searching find out God? — Job 11:7
Can you fathom the mystery of God? — Job 11:7

"Oh that I knew where I might find him!" — Job 23:3
Oh that I knew where I might find him! — Job 23:3

The Lord is nigh unto all them that call upon him, to all that call upon him in truth. Thy word is truth. — Psalm 145:18, John 17:17
Yahweh is near to all those who call on him, to all who call on him in truth. Your word is truth. — Psalm145:18, John 17:17

Him hath God exalted with his right hand to be a Prince and a Saviour, for to give repentance to Israel, and forgiveness of sins. — Acts 5:31
God exalted him with his right hand to be a Prince and a Savior, to give repentance to Israel, and remission of sins. — Acts 5:31

Behold, I, even I, will both search my sheep, and seek them out. — Ezekiel 34:11
Behold, I myself, even I, will search for my sheep, and will seek them out. — Ezekiel 34:11

THE POWER OF HIS LOVE

Yea, I have loved thee with an everlasting love: therefore with lovingkindness have I drawn thee. — Jeremiah 31:3

Yes, I have loved you with an everlasting love: therefore with loving kindness have I drawn you. — Jeremiah 31:3

And I, if I be lifted up from the earth, will draw all men unto me. — John 12:32
And I, if I am lifted up from the earth, will draw all people to myself. — John 12:32

And as Moses lifted up the serpent in the wilderness, even so must the Son of man be lifted up: that whosoever believeth in him should not perish, but have eternal life. — John 3:14-15
As Moses lifted up the serpent in the wilderness, even so must the Son of Man be lifted up, that whoever believes in him should not perish, but have eternal life. — John 3:14-15

> God loved the world so dearly that He gave His only-begotten Son that whosoever would accept Him might have power to live His righteous life.
> — 1SM 223

THE ONLY WAY

I am the way, the truth, and the life: no man cometh unto the Father, but by me.
— John 14:6
I am the way, the truth, and the life. No one comes to the Father, except through me. — John 14:6

No man can serve two masters. — Matthew 6:24
No one can serve two masters. — Matthew 6:24

Strait is the gate, and narrow is the way, which leadeth unto life, and few there be that find it. Strive to enter in at the strait gate. — Matthew 7:14, Luke 13:24
How narrow is the gate, and restricted is the way that leads to life! Few are those who find it. Strive to enter in by the narrow door. — Matthew 7:14, Luke 13:24

Neither is there salvation in any other: for there is none other name under heaven given among men, whereby we must be saved. — Acts 4:12
There is salvation in none other, for neither is there any other name under heaven, that is given among men, by which we must be saved! — Acts 4:12

GIFTS OF ENMITY AGAINST SIN AND DESIRE FOR GOODNESS

And I will put enmity between thee and the woman, and between thy seed and her seed: it shall bruise thy head, and thou shalt bruise his heel.
— Genesis 3:15

I will put enmity between you and the woman, and between your offspring and her offspring.
He will bruise your head, and you will bruise his heel.
— Genesis 3:15

That was the true Light, which lighteth every man that cometh into the world. — John 1:9
The true light that enlightens everyone was coming into the world. — John 1:9

> As through Christ every human being has life, so also through Him every soul receives some ray of divine light. Not only intellectual but spiritual power, a perception of right, a desire for goodness, exists in every heart. — Ed 29

> Desires for goodness and holiness are right: as far as they go, but if you stop here, they will avail nothing. — SC 48

The Creative Word

By the word of the Lord were the heavens made; and all the host of them by the breath of his mouth; . . . For he spake, and it was done; he commanded, and it stood fast.
— Psalm 33:6, 9

By Yahweh's word, the heavens were made; all their army by the breath of his mouth. . . . For he spoke, and it was done. He commanded, and it stood firm. — Psalm 33:6, 9

In the beginning was the Word, and the Word was with God, and the Word was God. All things were made by him: and without him was not any thing made that was made.
In him was life, and the life was the light of men.
But as many as received him,
to them gave he power to become the sons of God.
And the Word was made flesh, and dwelt among us.
— John 1:1, 3-4, 12, 14

In the beginning was the Word, and the Word was with God, and the Word was God. . . . All things were made through him. Without him was not anything made that has been made.
In him was life, and the life was the light of men. . . .
But as many as received him,
to them he gave the right to become God's children, . . .
The Word became flesh, and lived among us.
— John 1:1, 3-4, 12, 14

THE NEW BIRTH

Except a man be born again, he cannot see the kingdom of God. — John 3:3
Unless one is born anew, he can't see the Kingdom of God." — John 3:3

Which were born, not of blood, nor of the will of the flesh, nor of the will of man, but of God. — John 1:13
Who were born not of blood, nor of the will of the flesh, nor of the will of man, but of God. — John 1:13

Being born again, . . . by the word of God, which liveth and abideth forever. — 1 Peter 1:23
Having been born again, . . . through the word of God, which lives and remains forever. — 1 Peter 1:23

Except a man be born of water and of the Sprit, he cannot enter into the kingdom of God.
That which is born of the flesh is flesh: and that which is born of the Spirit is spirit. — John 3:5-6
Unless one is born of water and spirit, he can't enter into the Kingdom of God! That which is born of the flesh is flesh. That which is born of the Spirit is spirit. — John 3:5-6

Now are we the sons of God. . . . Whosoever is born of God sinneth not. . . . We shall be like him. — 1 John 3:2, 9
Now we are children of God. . . . Whoever is born of God doesn't commit sin, . . . We will be like him. — 1 John 3:2, 9

A New Creature

Create in me a clean heart, O God, and renew a right spirit within me. — Psalm 51:10
Create in me a clean heart, O God. Renew a right spirit within me. — Psalm 51:10

Lord, take my heart; for I cannot give it. . . .
Keep it pure, for I cannot keep it for Thee.
— COL 159

I delight to do thy will, O my God: yea, thy law is within my heart. . . . I will put my laws into their hearts, and in their minds will I write them. — Psalm 40:8, Hebrews 10:16
I delight to do your will, my God. Yes, your law is within my heart. . . . I will put my laws on their heart, I will also write them on their mind. — Psalm 40:8, Hebrews 10:16

*Therefore if any man be in Christ, he is a new creature: old things are passed away; behold, all things are become new.
— 2 Corinthians 5:17*
Therefore if anyone is in Christ, he is a new creation. The old things have passed away. Behold, all things have become new.
— 2 Corinthians 5:17

*There is therefore now no condemnation to them which are in Christ Jesus, who walk not after the flesh, but after the Spirit.
— Romans 8:1*
There is therefore now no condemnation to those who are in Christ Jesus, who don't walk according to the flesh but according to the Spirit. — Romans 8:1

Self on the Cross

*The good shepherd giveth
his life for the sheep.
— John 10:11*
The good shepherd lays
down his life for the sheep.
— John 10:11

*I am crucified with Christ.
— Galatians 2:20*
I have been crucified with
Christ. — Galatians 2:20

*If any man will come after me, let him deny himself, and take
up his cross daily, and follow me. — Luke 9:23*
If anyone desires to come after me, let him deny himself, take
up his cross, and follow me. — Luke 9:23

*He that findeth his life shall lose it; and he that loseth his life
for my sake shall find it. — Matthew 10:39*
He who seeks his life will lose it; and he who loses his life for
my sake will find it. — Matthew 10:39

*And if Christ be in you, the body is dead because of sin; but the
Spirit is life because of righteousness. — Romans 8:10*
If Christ is in you, the body is dead because of sin, but the
spirit is alive because of righteousness. — Romans 8:10

*Blessed are they which are persecuted for righteousness sake.
— Matthew 5:10*
Blessed are those who have been persecuted for righteousness' sake. — Matthew 5:10

My brethren, count it all joy when ye fall into divers temptations. — James 1:2
Count it all joy, my brothers, when you fall into various temptations. — James 1:2

A New Life

I am crucified with Christ; nevertheless I live; yet not I, but Christ liveth in me; and the life which I now live in the flesh I live by the faith of the Son of God, who loved me and gave himself for me.
— Galatians 2:20

I have been crucified with Christ, and it is no longer I that live, but Christ living in me. That life which I now live in the flesh, I live by faith in the Son of God, who loved me, and gave himself up for me. — Galatians 2:20

Here are they that keep the commandments of God, and the faith of Jesus. — Revelation 14:12
Here [are] those who keep the commandments of God, and the faith of Jesus. — Revelation 14:12

Therefore we are buried with him by baptism into death; that like as Christ was raised up from the dead by the glory of the Father, even so we also should walk in newness of life.
— Romans 6:4
We were buried therefore with him through baptism to death, that just like Christ was raised from the dead through the glory of the Father, so we also might walk in newness of life.
— Romans 6:4

For as many as are led by the Spirit of God, they are the sons of God. — Romans 8:14

For as many as are led by the Spirit of God, these are children of God. — Romans 8:14

These things write we unto you, that your joy may be full.
— 1 John 1:4

And we write these things to you, that our joy may be fulfilled. — 1 John 1:4

Heavenly Treasure

I counsel thee to buy of me gold tried in the fire, that thou mayest be rich, and white raiment, that thou mayest be clothed; and anoint thine eyes with eyesalve, that thou mayest see. — Revelation 3:18
I counsel you to buy from me gold refined by fire, that you may become rich; and white garments, that you may clothe yourself . . .; and eye salve to anoint your eyes, that you may see.
— Revelation 3:18

Thy word is a lamp unto my feet, and a light unto my path that the eyes of our understanding may be enlightened.
— Psalm 119:105, Ephesians 1:18
Your word is a lamp to my feet, and a light for my path having the eyes of your hearts enlightened.
— Psalm 119:105, Ephesians 1:18

That the trial of your faith, being much more precious than of gold that perisheth, though it be tried with fire, might be found unto praise and honour. — 1 Peter 1:7
That the proof of your faith, which is more precious than gold that perishes even though it is tested by fire, may be found to result in praise, glory, and honor. — 1 Peter 1:7

I put on righteousness, and it clothed me. — Job 29:14
I put on righteousness, and it clothed me. — Job 29:14

He hath clothed me with the garments of salvation, he hath covered me with the robe of righteousness. — Isaiah 61:10
He has clothed me with the garments of salvation, he has covered me with the robe of righteousness. — Isaiah 61:10

The Sustaining Word

Who being the brightness of his glory, and the express image of his person, and upholding all things by the word of his power, . . . sat down.
— *Hebrews 1:3*

His Son is the radiance of his glory, the very image of his substance, and upholding all things by the word of his power, . . . sat down. — Hebrews 1:3

Partakers of the divine nature. — 2 Peter 1:4
Partakers of the divine nature. — 2 Peter 1:4

I am the living bread. . . . Whoso eateth my flesh and drinketh my blood, hath eternal life; and I will raise him up at the last day. — John 6:51, 54
I am the living bread. . . . He who eats my flesh and drinks my blood has eternal life, and I will raise him up at the last day. — John 6:51, 54

The words that I speak unto you, they are spirit and they are life. — John 6:63
The words that I speak to you are spirit, and are life. — John 6:63

Take no thought for your life, what ye shall eat, or what ye shall drink; — Matthew 6:25

Therefore I tell you, don't be anxious for your life: what you will eat, or what you will drink. — Matthew 6:25

Which of you by taking thought can add one cubit to his stature? — Matthew 6:27
Which of you, by being anxious, can add one moment to his lifespan? — Matthew 6:27

And why take ye thought for raiment? Consider the lilies of the field, how they grow. — Matthew 6:28
Why are you anxious about clothing? Consider the lilies of the field, how they grow. — Matthew 6:28

Seek ye first the kingdom of God, and his righteousness, and all these things shall be added unto you. — Matthew 6:33
But seek first God's Kingdom, and his righteousness; and all these things will be given to you as well. — Matthew 6:33

Why are you anxious about clothing? Consider the lilies of the field, how they grow. — Matthew 6:28

The Mysteries

And upon her forehead was written, MYSTERY, BABYLON THE GREAT, THE MOTHER OF HARLOTS AND ABOMINATIONS OF THE EARTH. — Revelation 17:5

And on her forehead a name was written, "MYSTERY, BABYLON THE GREAT, THE MOTHER OF THE PROSTITUTES AND OF THE ABOMINATIONS OF THE EARTH." — Revelation 17:5

For the mystery of iniquity doth already work . . . with all deceivableness of unrighteousness in them that perish.
— 2 Thessalonians 2:7, 10
For the mystery of lawlessness already works . . . with all deception of wickedness for those who are being lost.
— 2 Thessalonians 2:7, 10

Great is the mystery of godliness. . . . In Him dwelleth all the fulness of the Godhead bodily. — 1 Timothy 3:16, Colossians 2:9
Without controversy, the mystery of godliness is great. . . . For in him all the fullness of the Godhead dwells bodily.
— 1 Timothy 3:16, Colossians 2:9

And of his fulness have we all received . . . that we may be filled with all the fulness of God. — John 1:16, Ephesians 3:19
From his fullness we all received . . . that you may be filled with all the fullness of God. — John 1:16, Ephesians 3:19

To whom God would make known . . . this mystery, . . . which is Christ in you, the hope of glory. — Colossians 1:27
To whom God was pleased to make known . . . this mystery, . . . which is Christ in you, the hope of glory.
— Colossians 1:27

And I looked, and, lo, a Lamb stood on the mount Sion, and with him an hundred and forty and four thousand, having the Father's name written in their foreheads. — Revelation 14:1
I saw, and behold, the Lamb standing on Mount Zion, and with him a number, one hundred forty-four thousand, having . . . the name of his Father written on their foreheads.
— Revelation 14:1

LIFE ETERNAL

And this is the record, that God hath given to us eternal life, and this life is in his Son. He that hath the Son hath life.
— *1 John 5:11-12*

The testimony is this, that God gave to us eternal life, and this life is in his Son. He who has the Son has the life.
— 1 John 5:11-12

I am the resurrection, and the life; he that believeth in me, though he were dead, yet shall he live; And whosoever liveth and believeth in me shall never die. Believest thou this?
— *John 11:25-26*

I am the resurrection and the life. He who believes in me will still live, even if he dies. Whoever lives and believes in me will never die. Do you believe this?
— John 11:25-26

> Satan could torture and kill the body, but he could not touch the life that was hid with Christ in God. — MB 30

Precious in the sight of the Lord is the death of His saints.
— *Psalm 116:15*

Precious in the sight of Yahweh is the death of his saints.
— Psalm 116:15

Yea, saith the Spirit, that they may rest from their labours; and their works do follow them. — *Revelation 14:13*
"Yes," says the Spirit, "that they may rest from their labors; for their works follow with them." — Revelation 14:13

The Rest

Come unto me all ye that labour, and are heavy laden, and I will give you rest. Take my yoke upon you, and learn of me, for I am meek and lowly in heart, and ye shall find rest unto your souls.
— Matthew 11:28-30

Come to me, all you who labor and are heavily burdened, and I will give you rest. Take my yoke upon you, and learn from me, for I am gentle and lowly in heart; and you will find rest for your souls. — Matthew 11:28-30

And on the seventh day God . . . rested . . . from all His work.
— Genesis 2:2
On the seventh day God . . . rested . . . from all his work.
— Genesis 2:2

There remaineth therefore a rest to the people of God. For he that is entered into his rest, he also hath ceased from his own works, as God did from his. — Hebrews 4:9-10
There remains therefore a Sabbath rest for the people of God. For he who has entered into his rest has himself also rested from his works, as God did from his. — Hebrews 4:9-10

The Father that dwelleth in me, he doeth the works. — John 14:10
But the Father who lives in me does his works. — John 14:10

He that abideth in me, and I in him, the same bringeth forth much fruit, for without me ye can do nothing. — John 15:5
He who remains in me, and I in him, the same bears much fruit, for apart from me you can do nothing. — John 15:5

The Light of Life

I am the light of the world; he that followeth me shall not walk in darkness, but shall have the light of life. — John 8:12
I am the light of the world. He who follows me will not walk in the darkness, but will have the light of life. — John 8:12

If we walk in the light as he is in the light, we have fellowship one with another, and the blood of Jesus Christ His Son cleanseth us from all sin. — 1 John 1:7
But if we walk in the light, as he is in the light, we have fellowship with one another, and the blood of Jesus Christ, his Son, cleanses us from all sin. — 1 John 1:7

Ye are the light of the world. — Matthew 5:14
You are the light of the world. — Matthew 5:14

We have also a more sure word of prophecy; whereunto ye do well that ye take heed, as unto a light that shineth in a dark place. — 2 Peter 1:19
We have the more sure word of prophecy; and you do well that you heed it, as to a lamp shining in a dark place.
— 2 Peter 1:19

And they overcame him by the blood of the Lamb, and by the word of their testimony. — Revelation 12:11
They overcame him because of the Lamb's blood, and because of the word of their testimony. — Revelation 12:11

The testimony of Jesus is the spirit of prophecy.
— Revelation 19:10
The testimony of Jesus is the Spirit of Prophecy.
— Revelation 19:10

Our Advocate

If any man sin, we have an advocate with the Father, Jesus Christ the righteous. — *1 John 2:1*
If anyone sins, we have a Counselor with the Father, Jesus Christ, the righteous. — 1 John 2:1

If we confess our sins, he is faithful and just to forgive us our sins, and to cleanse us from all unrighteousness. — *1 John 1:9*
If we confess our sins, he is faithful and righteous to forgive us the sins, and to cleanse us from all unrighteousness. — 1 John 1:9

For we have not an high priest which cannot be touched with the feelings of our infirmities; but was in all points tempted like as we are, yet without sin. — *Hebrews 4:15*
For we don't have a high priest who can't be touched with the feeling of our infirmities, but one who has been in all points tempted like we are, yet without sin. — Hebrews 4:15

Then shall the sanctuary be cleansed. — *Daniel 8:14*
Then shall the sanctuary be cleansed. — Daniel 8:14

For on that day shall the priest make an atonement for you to cleanse you, that ye may be clean from all your sins before the LORD. — *Leviticus 16:30*
For on this day shall atonement be made for you, to cleanse you; from all your sins you shall be clean before Yahweh. — Leviticus 16:30

THE REFRESHING

Repent ye therefore, and be converted, that your sins may be blotted out when the times of refreshing shall come from the presence of the Lord. — Acts 3:19

Repent therefore, and turn again, that your sins may be blotted out, so that there may come times of refreshing from the presence of the Lord. — Acts 3:19

And it shall come to pass afterward, that I will pour out my spirit upon all flesh; and your sons and your daughters shall prophesy. — Joel 2:28
It will happen afterward, that I will pour out my Spirit on all flesh; and your sons and your daughters will prophesy.
— Joel 2:28

*I will not leave you comfortless. The Father shall give you the Spirit of truth; for he dwelleth with you, and shall be in you.
— John 14:18, 16, 17 (paraphrased)*
I will not leave you orphans. The Father will give you another Counselor, for he lives with you, and will be in you.
— John 14:18, 16, 17 (paraphrased)

For as the rain cometh down . . . so shall my word be that goeth forth out of my mouth. — Isaiah 55:10, 11
For as the rain comes down . . . so shall my word be that goes forth out of my mouth. — Isaiah 55:10, 11

Victory

Know ye not that ye are the temple of God, and that the Spirit of God dwelleth in you? If any man defile the temple of God, him shall God destroy; for the temple of God is holy, which temple ye are.
— *1 Corinthians 3:16, 17*

Don't you know that you are a temple of God, and that God's Spirit lives in you? If anyone destroys the temple of God, God will destroy him; for God's temple is holy, which you are.
— 1 Corinthians 3:16, 17

He that saith, I know him, and keepeth not his commandments, is a liar. . . . He that saith he abideth in him ought himself to walk even as he walked. . . . He that saith he is in the light, and hateth his brother is in darkness even until now.
— *1 John 2:4, 6, 9*

One who says, "I know him," and doesn't keep his commandments, is a liar. . . . and the truth isn't in him. . . . [H]e who says he remains in him ought himself also to walk just like he walked. . . . .He who says he is in the light and hates his brother, is in the darkness even until now. — 1 John 2:4,6,9

Whosoever abideth in him sinneth not. — *1 John 3:6*
Whoever remains in him doesn't sin. — 1 John 3:6

Now unto him that is able to keep you from falling, and to present you faultless before the presence of his glory with exceeding joy. — *Jude 24*
Now to him who is able to keep them from stumbling, and to present you faultless before the presence of his glory in great joy. — Jude 24

The Final Victory

Flesh and blood cannot inherit the kingdom of God, neither doth corruption inherit incorruption...Behold I show you a mystery; We shall not all sleep, but we shall all be changed . . .

For this corruptible must put on incorruption, and this mortal shall put on immortality. . . .
O death, where is thy sting? O grave, where is thy victory? The sting of death is sin; But thanks be to God, which giveth us the victory through our Lord Jesus Christ.
— 1 Corinthains 15:50, 51, 53, 55-57

Now I say this, brothers, that flesh and blood can't inherit the Kingdom of God; neither does corruption inherit incorruption...Behold, I tell you a mystery. We will not all sleep, but we will all be changed... For this corruptible must put on incorruption, and this mortal must put on immortality... "Death, where is your sting? Hades, where is your victory?" The sting of death is sin. . . . But thanks be to God, who gives us the victory through our Lord Jesus Christ.
— 1 Corinthians 15:50, 51, 53, 55-57

THANKS BE UNTO GOD FOR HIS UNSPEAKABLE GIFT.
— 2 Corinthians 9:15
NOW THANKS BE TO GOD FOR HIS UNSPEAKABLE GIFT! — 2 Corinthians 9:15

Dear Reader,

Most of the references in this booklet are taken from Scripture, but several quotations are by Ellen G. White, Betty Nick's favorite spiritual writer. Ellen White was a major figure in the early history of the Seventh-day Adventist Church. She experienced visions and had an extraordinary and ongoing personal experience with the Lord. These quotations are not intended to point to any particular denomination, but to encourage all who seek God's presence in their lives. Both the compiler and the publisher believe that Christians of all denominations, in fact, any seekers after truth, can benefit from becoming acquainted with Ellen White's experience and writings.

The title of this book is taken from one of Ellen White's books, *Thoughts from the Mount of Blessing*, where she said:

> Righteousness is holiness, likeness to God, and "God is love." (1 John 4:16). It is conformity to the law of God, for "all Thy commandments are righteousness" (Psalm 119:172), and "love is the fulfilling of the law" (Romans 13:10). Righteousness is love, and love is the light and the life of God. The righteousness of God is embodied in Christ. We receive righteousness by receiving Him (p. 18).

Betty Nick, Compiler
Henry Neufeld, Publisher

The following Ellen White books are quoted:

Steps to Christ (SC)
Thoughts from the Mount of Blessing (MB)
Selected Messages, Volume 1 (1SM)
Education (Ed)
Christ's Object Lessons (COL)

www.ingramcontent.com/pod-product-compliance
Lightning Source LLC
Chambersburg PA
CBHW040314050426
42452CB00018B/2843